"Einat Mazor rolled up her sle͟ and casein problems. Now she shares all h͟ you follow a gluten-free, casein-free diet, this͟ i Gluten Free living magazine, Ann Whelan).

"I am honored that Einat asked me to write about her cookbook. In reality it is much more than just a cookbook.

Einat has been able to bring together all of these essentials into recipes that not only nourish the body but also the soul. She has incorporated many of the gluten free and dairy free ingredients into family and holiday favorites. These recipes are ones that the entire family can enjoy – from helping in the preparation to savoring every bite at the table. The recipes include practical everyday meals as well as special dishes for holidays and family celebrations. These are the cornerstone of a gluten free dairy free diet.

My heart felt thanks to Einat for creating not only such a fabulous book but for also sharing her talents and inspiration with others." (Anne Lee, MSEd, RD, LD is presently the Director of Nutritional Services for Schar USA, international leading specialist in gluten-free dietary products. Lee was formerly a nutritionist with the Celiac Disease Center at Columbia University, and is a respected authority on celiac disease and gluten intolerance).

"One size does not fit all in the world of autism. There is no universal therapy, treatment or diet that addresses all issues for all people. Yet many individuals have real allergies and sensitivities to wheat, gluten, dairy and casein. Einat Mazor, through her own journey with her daughter's celiac disease, has created a collection of simple, delicious recipes that you will want to make because they are so incredibly good. If you also happen to have sensitivities to gluten and dairy, then this is the book for you!" (Jed Baker, Ph.D., Author of No More Meltdowns, Social Skills Training for Children and Adolescents with Aspergers Syndrome and Social Communication Problems and several other titles.).

"It's all about flavor. When your choices are limited due to gluten and lactose intolerance you don't want to lose the fun of flavorful foods. Einat's recipes keep the flavor intact. Her simple substitutions mean that delicious and tasty meals are easy to make. No one wants bland - and these recipes use creative doses of spices to make dishes so delicious that even the non-allergic family members will enjoy them and miss nothing of the forbidden foods .Einat's book has creative seasoning and allergen-friendly substitutes which help to create flavorful dishes." (Susan Goodstadt-Levin Co-Leader, Northern New Jersey Celiac Support Group).

Mastering your Gluten & Dairy free kitchen

Easy Recipes, Chef's Tips, and the Best Products for your Pantry

By Einat Mazor

iUnivers, Inc. Bloomington

MASTERING YOUR GLUTEN AND DAIRY FREE KITCHEN
Easy Recipes, Chef's Tips, and the Best Products for Your Pantry

iUniverse Star
an iUniverse, Inc. imprint

iUniverse books may be ordered through booksellers or by contacting:

iUniverse
1663 Liberty Drive
Bloomington, IN 47403
www.iuniverse.com
1-800-Authors (1-800-288-4677)

Because of the dynamic nature of the Internet, any Web addresses or links
contained in this book may have changed since publication and may no longer
be valid. The views expressed in this work are solely those of the author and
do not necessarily reflect the views of the publisher, and the publisher hereby
disclaims any responsibility for them.

ISBN: 978-1-936236-49-7 (pbk)
ISBN: 978-1-936236-50-3 (ebk)

Library of Congress Control Number: 2011902613

Printed in the United States of America
iUniverse rev. date: 6/8/2011

Contents

Acknowledgments

This book was made possible thanks to the assistance of many talented people but most of all I would like to thank my husband for his love and patience during this writing process.

I would also like to thank my friends at the Natural Gourmet Institute for Food and Health in New York City for giving me their support, care and important input.

To Dr.Charles Saha, Ruti, Eileen, for their knowledge and friendship.

Last but not least to Edan, Jonathan and Roy my beautiful children and my biggest fans.

I love you and your gracious spirits.

Preface

Food has always been a big part of my life. I remember myself as a child looking at my mom's cookbooks, standing in the kitchen and teaching my dolls how to cook. That passion for food passed on to the next generation. From their early days, my children grew in an environment that appreciates and enjoys food.

Around her third birthday, I noticed that Edan, my daughter, was short for her age and that she was not gaining weight in spite of her healthy appetite. She also needed to go to the bathroom after each meal. At the time, I just thought that she had inherited her father's frame and fast metabolism.

When Edan turned four, I noticed that she was not growing fast enough and that her height was in the fifth percentile for her age group. Her pediatrician assured me that there was no cause for concern as long as she stayed on the chart. Her annual physical at age five again indicated insufficient growth, but her pediatrician accused me of being overprotective when I voiced my anxiety. I insisted on a deeper investigation, which included hormone screening and bone age tests, but all results came back normal.

By Edan's sixth birthday, I felt that something was seriously wrong, but I did not understand how to help her or what questions to ask her doctor. All I knew was that she was not growing and that she just didn't look right for a girl her age.

Our pediatrician, who still did not appear to be taking my concerns seriously, referred us to an endocrinologist. The results of my daughter's blood tests led him to suspect celiac disease. An endoscope biopsy, conducted under anesthesia, confirmed his diagnosis. This information allowed us to make the dietary changes that improved our lives. Our daughter has grown and looks healthy. I rolled up my sleeves to start off our new journey of exploring the vast possibilities of gluten- and dairy-free food.

As a caterer and a chef, I was determined to bring to our family table the same flavors and aromas that we enjoyed before my daughter's diagnosis changed our eating habits. We love good food, and there was no reason we had to be deprived of this pleasure.

This book offers recipes that are easy to prepare for everyday cooking and baking. So choose your first recipe, and go for it with love and joy!

 Chef's Cooking Tip

The information is provided for general use and should not form the basis of a medical diagnosis or treatment plan. It is very important to consult with your doctor about your specific diet and condition.

The Gluten and Dairy Free Diet: Why and For Whom?

Gluten is a protein found in wheat, rye, spelt, barley, and other grains. Individuals with sensitivity to gluten may have celiac disease, an intolerance in which gluten sets off an autoimmune reaction that causes the destruction of the villi, hairlike protrusions lining the small intestine. Without healthy villi, a person becomes malnourished no matter how much food gets into his or her body.

According to a study by the University of Maryland School of Medicine in Baltimore, celiac disease affects one in 133 Americans. At least three million Americans have celiac disease and need to adhere to a gluten-free diet. Gluten intolerance can also affect people with other autoimmune diseases such as thyroid disease, systemic lupus, erythema-tosus, type 1 diabetes, liver disease, collagen vascular disease, rheumatoid arthritis, and Sjogren's syndrome. Individuals suffering from these conditions may benefit from the gluten-free diet.

Dairy allergy, like any food allergy, may trigger a wide array of symptoms. Dairy includes all types of cow milk, cheese, butter, cream, yogurt, cottage cheese, and ice cream, though this list is not exhaustive. It also includes the proteins casein, whey, and lactalbumin, which are found in many processed foods. Low-fat and nonfat milk are just as allergenic as whole milk.

An ELISA food allergy panel to detect dairy antibodies, performed with a simple blood test, can diagnose a milk allergy. The dairy allergy can include symptoms such as sinusitis, heartburn or acid reflux, constipation, diarrhea, irritable bowel syndrome, arthritis, autism, and childhood ear infections. Some people find that a gluten and casein (a protein found in milk and dairy products) free diet is beneficial for children with autism.

A 2007 report by the Centers for Disease Control and Prevention found that one in every 150 American children has an autism spectrum disorder. Approximately 1.5 million Americans and their families are affected.

Protective Steps to Avoid Gluten and Dairy in Your Diet

- Learn to read food labels carefully. Be especially alert to the presence of modified food starch, hydrolyzed plant and vegetable protein, and soy sauce; they may contain gluten.

- Have a toaster and some bake ware that is dedicated solely to your gluten-free foods. This ensures that they remain free from contamination by forbidden ingredients.

- When dining out, be prepared. Call the restaurant in advance with your questions about the menu.

- Remember that you can always request to speak to a restaurant's chef or manager to ask about the food preparation. (Is the oil used for French fries only, or is it also used to fry floured items, such as chicken tenders? What are the ingredients of the marinade?)

- When traveling, contact your hotel. Some lodging establishments will accommodate your special needs.

My Product Pantry

I learned that not only is it necessary to experiment when exploring gluten and dairy free food preparation, it's also important to master your pantry.

There are so many products available now, some of them better then others and most of them expensive. You need to know what to buy. Most of the products can be found at supermarkets like Whole Foods Market, which stocks organic and natural goods, or online at www.glutenfreemall.com and www.glutenfree.com. You may also be surprised that a lot of the products are available in your everyday supermarket. Look in the aisles that contain organic, Asian, or Kosher foods.

The following lists of products are worth the investment, and once you have them, or at least some of them, you are set for cooking, baking, and snacking.

Cereal, Breads, and Milk Products

-EnviroKidz cold cereals (my kids' favorite)

-corn flakes and maple buckwheat flakes—Arrowhead Mills

-gluten- and dairy-free breads—Whole Foods Market

-breads, buns, rolls, and bread crumbs—Schaer (www.schaer.com)

-bread sticks—Glutino (www.glutino.com)

-bagels and granola—Enjoy Life Natural Brands (www.enjoylifenb.com)

-oatmeal—Bob's Red Mill Certified Rolled Oats, -Gifts Of Nature
 (www. giftsofnature.net)

-rice milk—Rice Dream

-almond milk—Blue Diamond

-soy milk

-an alternative to dry milk powder—Vance's DariFree
 (www.vancesfoods.com)

-Yogurt—Soy Delicious (soy based), So -Delicious (coconut milk based)

-cream cheese alternative—Tofutti's regular and garlic flavors

Granola, Spreads, and Pancake Mixes

-fruit jams, jellies, and fruit preserves

-Granola—Enjoy Life Brand, Bakery On Main

-parve chocolate spread—Hashahar (Kosher aisle in the supermarket)

-Pitted pressed dates—Galil-Kosher aisle

-pancake mixes—Bob's Red Mill (www.bobsredmill.com)

-waffles and mini waffles—Van's All Natural

Tortillas and Rice Paper

-corn tortillas—Goya

-rice paper

-spring roll wrappers—Blue Dragon

-authentic pad thai—Thai Pavilion (Asian aisle in the supermarket)

Baking Products

-cocoa powder—Hershey's

-Natural sweetner—agave nectar, maple sugar, brown sugar

-xanthan gum—Bob's Red Mill

-baking powder

-baking soda

-vanilla extract

-almond extract

-lemon extract

-gluten- and dairy-free chocolate chips—Enjoy Life Natural Brands

-gluten-free baking flours—Bob's Red Mill

-gluten-free flours: garbanzo flour, white rice flour, brown rice flour,
buckwheat flour, tapioca flour, sorghum flour, quinoa flour, millet flour, corn
flour

-baking spray made with olive oil or canola oil

-margarine

-vegetable shortening—Crisco

-natural and artificial colors and flavors

-modified food starch is made from corn if the product is made in the
United States

-yeast

Broth, Spices, Pastes, and Sauces

-bread crumbs——Gillian's foods
-organic chicken broth—Imagine, Pacific, Amy's
-organic chicken powder—Vogue
-spices—McCormick, Penzeys Spices(www.penzeys.com)
-dry herbs— basil, parsley, oregano, thyme, dill
-oils— olive oil, extra virgin olive oil, canola oil, coconut oil—all are safe
-organic ketchup
-mustard
-tomato paste
-crushed tomatoes
-soy sauce—La Choy
-mirin—sweet Japanese cooking wine
-tamarind paste
-umeboshi paste(www.edenfoods.com)
-miso—white, red (www.edenfoods.com)
-marinara—Newman's, Rau

Vinegars

-plain vinegar
-apple cider vinegar
-rice vinegar
-balsamic vinegar
 (Never use malt vinegar!)

Pastas and Grains

-pasta—Tinkyada, Glutano
-spaghetti—Notta Pasta
-bean threads—KA-ME
-quinoa
-quinoa flakes—Quinoa Ancient Harvest
-corn
-amaranth
-whole buckwheat grouts—Wolff's
-rice, all types
-wild rice
-beans, all types

Nuts, Dry Fruits, and Snacks

-nuts

-sesame seeds

-tahini paste

-dried fruits

-pretzels—Glutino, Ener-G (www.ener-g.com), Barkat

-rice cakes, salted or plain—Lundberg

-chips—Frito-Lay, Kettle, Utz, Wise

-marshmallows - plain

-brown rice marshmallow treats—Glenny's (www.glennys.com)

-KinniTOOS chocolate or vanilla sandwich cookies—Kinnikinnick foods
(www.kinnikinnick.com)

cookies—Enjoy Life Natural Brands

-cocoa loco snack bars—Enjoy Life Natural Brands

-meringues (not chocolate flavored)—Miss Meringue
(www.missmeringue.com)

-plain popcorn

-parve ice cream (www.kosher.com/store)

-ice cream—So Delicious

-whipped soy topping—Soya too!

-nondairy whipped topping—Rich's or Kineret
(www.kosher.com/store)

Bakeware

-silicone muffin sheet

-silicone baking trays

-silicone loaf pan

-paper muffin liners

Beverages

- ice tea mixes
- sports drinks
- coffee
- distilled alcohol(rum, vodka, gin, whiskey)
- sherry
- Wine
- champagne
- beer—Bard's Tale Beer company (Golden Sorghum Lager), Budweiser (Redbridge)
- honey beer—Ramapo Valley Brewery

Always avoid these gluten-containing ingredients: rye, malt, bran, bulgur, couscous, durum, farina, faro, graham flour, kamout, matzo meal, orzo, panko crumbs, semolina, seitan, spelt, triticale, udon, and wheat.

 Chef's Cooking Tip

Passover is a great time to visit local supermarkets to find a large variety of kosher gluten-free items: cakes, cookies, cereals, and pancake mixes. You can usually stock your pantry easily and for a very reasonable price.

Nutritional Information about the Products

Tahini is a great calcium supplement for a dairy-free diet.

Quinoa is a high protein grain known as an ancient grain.

Almond milk can be use as a dairy substitute that is high in protein, calcium, and good fats.

Chickpea flour is a good source of zinc, folate, and protein. Chickpeas are very high in dietary fiber. Chickpeas are a significant source of calcium (190 mg/100 g) that some sources quote as equal to that of yogurt and close to that of milk.

Sweet white sorghum flour (also known as sweet sorghum or jowar) makes an excellent wheat flour substitute in quick-leavened baked goods such as muffins or loaf bread. Sorghum flour is ground from the sorghum plant (used to make sorghum syrup). It is best combined with a gluten-free starch, such as cornstarch or tapioca. Tapioca flour is ground from cassava roots; it is the same tapioca as in tapioca pearls or tapioca pudding.

White rice flour is close to wheat flour in taste and consistency. It lacks any binding ability, however, and works best when combined with other flours and starches in baked goods.

Sweet rice and white rice flour are finer than brown rice flour, although mills are now producing fine brown rice flours for the gluten-free market. Choose the finest grind possible for gluten-free baking; coarser grinds are slightly gritty.

Brown rice flour is a whole grain flour with a higher protein content than white rice flours. Sweet rice flour can be used as a thickener in gravies. Other higher protein gluten-free flours include quinoa, buckwheat, soy, and amaranth.

Xanthan gum is a natural thickener, emulsifier, and stabilizer produced from the fermentation of corn sugar. It is the most popular binding agent, but others can be used too, including kuzu powder, guar gum, carob (locust bean) gum, and gelatin. These agents are often used in combination with each other.

Miso is a fermented soybean paste. It can be used instead of salt or soy sauce. It has medicinal properties.

Umeboshi paste is a paste made from pickled umeboshi plum, fermented sour plum.

About Parve or Pareve Ingredients

You can find parve or pareve products, which are also always kosher (foods that are approved by Jewish law), in almost every big supermarket. The parve or pareve designations signal that a product is free of dairy derivatives and casein. None of the equipment in the manufacturing line is contaminated with the residue of dairy ingredients.

Look for the parve symbol, a capital or lowercase letter k circumscribed by a circle or a star, or the written words on the package.

Breakfast

Corn Cakes

Breakfast

Have a little sunshine in the morning or in between meals. You can wrap these wonderful yellow corn cakes individually and freeze them.

You can use peas, broccoli, or spinach if you are sensitive to corn.

What do you need?
(Makes about 12 corn cakes)

1 (11 oz.) can kernel corn or 1½ cups of frozen kernel corn, thawed
1 cup soy milk or other milk substitute
3 eggs
3 tablespoons canola oil
3 tablespoons gluten-free baking flour
½ teaspoon baking powder
1 teaspoon salt
½ teaspoon black pepper
1 cup cheddar or mozzarella cheese substitute, grated

How to make?

- Preheat the oven to 350°F.
- Mix all the ingredients together in a medium size bowl.
- Spray canola oil onto an 8-inch loaf pan or into 12 muffins cups lined with paper cups, filling each to three-quarter capacity
- Pour the batter into the pan or cups.
- Sprinkle with grated cheese.
- Bake for 30 minutes or until golden brown.

Cheesy Popovers

When I have guests coming over, this is the one recipe that never fails. Served on a platter of dry fruits and vegetables, the result always look fabulous and makes everyone (even mothers~in~ law) feel good inside.

What do you need?

(Makes about 24 popovers)

3 eggs
1 cup soy milk or other milk substitute
¾ cup gluten-free baking flour
¾ cup dairy-free grated cheese
3 tablespoons canola oil
½ teaspoon ground black pepper
½ teaspoon dry basil or dry oregano
¼ teaspoon salt

How to make?

- Preheat oven to 350°F.
- Mix all the ingredients together in a medium size bowl.
- Spray the muffin sheet with canola oil.
- Pour the batter into the muffin cups, filling each to three-quarter capacity.
- Bake for 20 minutes, until golden brown and puffed up.

Cinnamon French Toast

It all started with a brown bag. I was standing in the kitchen making my famous French toast, with my kids pulling on my clothes and begging to help me cook. With a little smile I handed each a brown bag and taught them how to shake, shake, shake. Who would have thought that such a simple idea would become a family tradition?

What do you need?

(Serves 4–6)

6 slices of gluten- and dairy-free bread

2 eggs

3 cups soy milk or other milk substitute, vanilla flavored

3 tablespoons canola oil

2 teaspoons cinnamon

1 tablespoon sugar

1 brown paper bag

How to make?

- Beat the eggs in one bowl.
- Pour milk into a second bowl.
- Dip one slice of bread into the milk, coating first one side and then the other.
- Repeat the dipping process using the egg mixture. Follow the same steps with the rest of the bread slices.
- Pour canola oil into a frying pan. Warm the oil for 30 seconds before placing the bread in the pan. Each slice should be fried separately.
- Fry the bread on a medium-high heat, cooking each side for 3–4 minutes.
- While the bread is hot, slice it into triangles or 1½-inch-wide sticks.
- Mix the sugar and the cinnamon in a brown bag.
- Place the bread in the bag. Fold the bag and shake it. You may need to do two batches.
- Serve warm with fresh fruit salad or dairy-free whipped cream.

Noodle Casserole

This is a perfect dish for pasta leftovers. Don't skip the grated apples, as they add sweetness and richness to this casserole. My family and I like to enjoy this fulfilling and sweet recipe at breakfast.

What do you need?

(Serves 6–8)

1 package of cooked gluten-free rice pasta (elbow pasta or any other short pasta)

2 sticks of margarine, room temperature

4 eggs

1 cup sugar

2 (6 oz.) containers of plain or vanilla dairy-free yogurt

½ package of dairy-free cream cheese, such as Tofutti, at room temperature

1 teaspoon cinnamon

½ cup grated apples

3 tablespoons raisins

How to make?

- Preheat oven to 375°F.
- Mix the margarine, eggs, sugar, 2 yogurt containers, cheese, cinnamon, apples, and raisins in a large bowl.
- Add the cooked pasta to the bowl.
- Pour the mixture into a 9" x 9" greased baking dish and bake for 30–45 minutes, or until the top is golden brown.

Cheesy Tortillas

One day my daughter craved pizza. I didn't have gluten and dairy free pizza dough in my freezer, so I needed to improvise. I found that corn tortillas are the best solution. You can cut the prepared tortillas into triangles with a pizza roller and dip them in your favorite sauce.

What do you need?

(Serves 3)

6 corn tortillas

2 cups grated mozzarella cheese substitute

1 tablespoon canola oil

How to make?

- Warm the oil in a frying pan for 30 seconds.
- Place one tortilla in the pan and sprinkle cheese over it, then top it with another tortilla.
- Fry the tortilla for 12 minutes, then flip it and fry the remaining side for 1 minute.
- Repeat the process for all the tortillas and cut into triangles.

Chocolate Muffins

Get your morning off to a good start with a cup of tea and this delicious muffin. Its fluffy texture is great.

What do you need?

(Makes about 12 Muffins)

1 cup brown rice flour

½ cup + 2 tablespoons of sweet white sorghum flour

½ cup buckwheat flour

1½ teaspoons baking soda

2 teaspoons baking powder

½ teaspoon salt

2 teaspoons xanthan gum

1 cup warm rice milk

½ cup warm water

¾ cup agave nectar

1 teaspoon vanilla extract

3 eggs, beaten in a small bowl

1 cup canola oil

½ cup gluten and dairy-free chocolate chips

How to make?

- Preheat oven to 350°F.
- Lightly oil a 12 muffins tin lined with paper cups.
- Sift together the flours, baking soda, baking powder, salt, and xanthan gum in a large bowl and set it aside.
- In a separate large bowl, combine the wet ingredients: water, agave nectar, vanilla extract, eggs, and canola oil.
- Using a rubber spatula, fold the dry ingredients into the wet ingredients in 3 parts, alternating it with adding the rice milk in 2 parts. Mix until thoroughly combined.
- Fold in the chocolate chips. Don't over mix the batter.
- Fill the cups three-quarters full with batter.
- Bake for 25–30 minutes or until a toothpick inserted comes out clean.
- Cool the muffins in the pan on a rack.

My Ultimate Blueberry Muffins

The lemon accentuates the blueberry flavor and adds lightness to the recipe. This is truly the ultimate muffin!

What do you need?

(Makes about 12 muffins)

1 cup rice flour
1 cup + 2 tablespoons of sweet white sorghum flour
1½ teaspoons baking soda
2 teaspoons baking powder
½ teaspoon salt
2 teaspoons xanthan gum
½ cup fresh or frozen blueberries
½ cup warm water
¾ cup agave nectar
juice from a half-squeezed lemon
1 teaspoon lemon zest
3 eggs, beaten in a small bowl
1 cup canola oil
1 cup warm rice milk or soy milk

How to make?

- Preheat oven to 350°F.
- Lightly oil a 12 muffins tin lined with paper cups.
- Sift together the flours, baking soda, baking powder, salt, and xanthan gum in a large bowl.
- Add the blueberries, toss gently, and set aside the bowl.
- In a separate large bowl, combine the wet ingredients: water, agave nectar, lemon juice, lemon zest, eggs, and canola oil.
- Using a rubber spatula, fold the dry ingredients into the wet ingredients in 3 parts, alternating it with adding the rice milk in 2 parts. Mix until thoroughly combined.
- Fill the cups three-quarters full with batter.
- Bake for 25–30 minutes or until a toothpick inserted comes out clean.
- Cool muffins in the pan on a rack.

Apple Muffins

Many muffins look delicious but end up being dry. I love this recipe, because the applesauce and the apples add flavor and moisture.

What do you need?
(Makes about 12 muffins)

1 cup white rice flour
¼ cup sweet white sorghum flour
1 teaspoons cinnamon
1½ teaspoons baking soda
½ teaspoon salt
¼ teaspoon xanthan gum
1 cup sweetened applesauce
1 egg
¾ cup sugar
3 tablespoons canola oil
1 cup cubed, peeled golden delicious apples (about 1¼ apples)
1/3 cup soy milk or other milk substitute

How to make?

- Preheat oven to 375°F and lightly oil a muffin sheet.
- Sift together the flours, cinnamon, baking soda, salt, and xanthan gum in a large bowl, and set it aside.
- In a separate bowl, combine the applesauce, egg, sugar, and canola oil.
- Using a rubber spatula, fold the dry mixture into the applesauce mixture in 3 parts, alternating with adding the soy milk in 2 parts. Mix until thoroughly combined.
- Fold in the cubed apples. Don't overmix the batter. You want the muffins to be fluffy and not dense.
- Divide the batter evenly into the muffin tins.
- Bake for about 25 minutes or until golden brown. Cool muffins in the pan on a rack.

Chef's Cooking Tip

Muffins are best enjoyed on the same day they are baked, while they are still fresh and fluffy, but you can also store them in the refrigerator in an airtight container. When you are ready to indulge, just warm them at 350°F for 5–7 minutes.

Salads and Appetizers

Salad Greens with Avocado and Cucumber

I prepared this dish in one of my cooking classes, and everybody loved it. The salad is both crunchy and smooth.

What do you need?
(Serves 4–6)

2 (7 oz.) packages of salad greens
1 sliced avocado
½ English cucumber, sliced
3 sliced green onions
¼ cup fresh lemon juice
½ cup extra virgin olive oil
1 teaspoon of minced garlic
1 teaspoon salt
½ teaspoon ground black pepper

How to make?

- In a big bowl, mix the greens, avocado, cucumber, and green onions.
- In a small bowl, mix the lemon juice, garlic, salt, and pepper.
- Slowly add in the olive oil to the small bowl to make the vinaigrette.
- Just before serving, mix the vinaigrette into the big bowl of salad.

Arugula Salad with Pears and Roasted Walnuts

I love to use fruits in my salads; pears are sweet and have a great texture. You can prepare the salad ahead of time and pour on the vinaigrette just before serving.

What do you need?

(Serves 4–6)

For the vinaigrette:
1 finely minced shallot
1 teaspoon Dijon mustard
2 teaspoons red wine vinegar
¼ cup extra virgin olive oil
1 teaspoon sugar
1 teaspoon honey
salt and pepper to taste

For the salad:

1 (7oz.) bag of prewashed arugula
3 pears, peeled and sliced
½ cup roasted walnuts, crushed

How to make?

- Combine the shallot, mustard, vinegar, oil, sugar, honey, salt, and pepper.
- Toss the arugula, pears, and roasted walnuts with the vinaigrette for taste.

Cabbage Salad with Pine Nuts and Sliced Almonds

This is a delicious Asian flavored salad that goes well with fish and beef. This is one of the few salads that are just as good eaten the day after.

What do you need?

(Serves 4–6)

2 (16oz.) bags of coleslaw salad or 1 head of a medium sized cabbage, shredded
1/3 cup pine nuts roasted
1/3 cup roasted sliced almonds
1/3 cup sugar
1/3 cup vinegar
1/3 cup canola oil

How to make?

- In a saucepan, heat the sugar, vinegar, and oil until the sugar dissolves.
- Allow the mixture to cool.
- In a large bowl, pour the sauce mixture over the cabbage, and mix well.
- Sprinkle the almonds and pine nuts on top.

Spring Salad with Orange-Mandarin and Sunflower Seeds

I love to serve this salad as an appetizer. The simplicity and the colors of the salad are what it's all about.

What do you need?
(Serves 4–6)

2 (10oz.) bags of iceberg lettuce
1 (8oz.) container of orange-mandarin
2 tablespoons of chopped green onions (only the green parts)
¼ cup fresh lemon juice
2 tablespoons juice from the orange-mandarin
2 teaspoons light brown sugar
1 teaspoon salt
ground black pepper
½ cup extra virgin olive oil
2 tablespoons roasted sunflower seeds

How to make?

- In a big bowl, mix the lettuce, orange-mandarin segments, and green onions.
- In a small bowl, mix the lemon juice, orange-mandarin juice, sugar, salt, and pepper.
- Slowly add the olive oil to the small bowl to make the vinaigrette.
- Just before serving, add the vinaigrette and the seeds to the salad.

Chinese Spring Roll Wrappers

Rice wrappers make a great appetizer. Fill them with vegetables or rice and you are good to go. Served cold or warm, they're a great party food.

What do you need?
(Serves 4–6)

12 spring roll wrappers
1(16oz.) bag of coleslaw salad
1 small onion, cubed
1 minced garlic clove
½ cup shredded cooked chicken
3 tablespoons gluten-free soy sauce
1 tablespoon mirin (sweet Japanese cooking wine)
½ teaspoon salt
½ teaspoon ground black pepper

For the sweet chili dipping sauce:

3 tablespoons rice vinegar
¼ cup gluten-free soy sauce
2 tablespoons honey
1 teaspoon grated ginger
1 teaspoon crushed red pepper

How to make?

To prepare the filling:

- In a large sauté pan, sauté the onion for 3 minutes.
- Add the garlic and sauté for another 1 minute.
- Add the coleslaw salad, and cook for 5 additional minutes.
- Add the chicken, soy sauce, mirin, salt, and pepper, and cook for another 3 minutes.
- Allow the mixture to cool.
- Prepare the dipping sauce by mixing together the vinegar, soy sauce, honey, ginger, and pepper. Set aside.

Working with spring roll wrappers:

- Pour warm water into a shallow baking tray.
- Dip, one at a time, the wrappers into the water for 15–20 seconds, or until they are soft and pliable.
- Lay the wrappers flat over a clean, straight surface.
- Place filling in the center of the wrapper, and fold the ends toward the center. Gently roll the other two ends like a jelly roll. Cut the rolls in half, and lay on a serving plate
- Mix the ingredients for the sweet chili dipping sauce, and serve.

Herb and Cheese Latkes

When I crave comfort food, I cook these earthy, crunchy, flavorful patties. I love them with my favorite dairy-free yogurt.

What do you need?
(Serves 6–8)

6 cups of chopped mixed herbs (basil, Italian parsley, cilantro, dill)

1 cup grated mozzarella cheese substitute

1 large potato, peeled and shredded

4 tablespoons gluten-free breadcrumbs

5 eggs

2 teaspoons salt

1 teaspoon ground pepper

canola oil

How to make?

- In a big bowl, mix the ingredients together.
- Pour ½ inch of canola oil into a frying pan and heat over medium-high heat.
- With clean hands, using a tablespoon, mold the mixture into flat, oval-shaped patties.
- Fry for about 3-4 minutes per side, or until golden brown.

Chef's Cooking Tip

For extra crunch, place the shredded potatoes in a dry, clean towel and squeeze well to get all the liquids out. Freeze the cheese for about 20 minutes for easier grating.

Tempura Vegetables

Even today, I can still hear my mother's voice echoing "Eat your veggies!" As a caterer, I am always looking for new approaches when it comes to vegetables, because I know that we all have moms.

What do you need?

(Serves 4–6)

For the tempura batter:

1½ cup white rice flour

1 tablespoon arrowroot flour

1 cup icy cold club soda

1 teaspoon sweet paprika

1 teaspoon salt

5 stalks asparagus with ends trimmed

2 cups green beans

2 zucchini sliced ¼-inch thick

1 sweet potato sliced ¼-inch thick

canola oil, for frying

For the Asian-style dipping sauce:

½ cup organic smooth peanut butter

3 tablespoons rice vinegar

¼ cup mirin

1 teaspoon sugar

1 teaspoon grated ginger

1 teaspoon crushed red pepper

How to make?

- In a cold mixing bowl, mix the rice flour, arrowroot flour, club soda, paprika, and salt until it reaches the consistency of pancake batter.
- Using a deep pan or a wok, heat about 2 inches of oil to 375°F.

- Dry the vegetables well, and then dip them into in the batter one at a time and fry for about 2 minutes, or until golden brown.
- Place the fried pieces place on a paper towel to absorb excess oil.
- Prepare the dipping sauce by mixing the ingredients together until it reaches a smooth, thick consistency.

Chef's Cooking Tip:

This tempura batter is great; I love to entertain with this dish. I cut all the vegetables the day before cooking, so I will only need to dip and fry them on the day of my guests' arrival.

The Main Course

Salmon with Mochi and Pesto

I was glad to discover mochi in the frozen foods aisle of my local Natural store. Mochi is a traditional Japanese food made from sweet rice. When baked, it puffs up. You can find it in two flavors: plain and sweet. In this recipe, I'm using the plain flavor, which complements savory dishes.

What do you need?

(Serves 4)

16 pieces (2 packages) of plain mochi cut into 1–2 inch squares

4 pieces of salmon, 1 ounce each, seasoned with salt and pepper

¼ cup chopped pistachios

¼ cup pesto sauce(check the next page for the recipe)

4 tablespoons chopped Italian parsley

salt

ground black pepper

How to make?

- Preheat the oven to 400°F.
- Arrange the salmon on a baking sheet, making sure the pieces do not touch.
- Sprinkle each piece of fish with 1 tablespoon pistachios.
- Bake for 10 minutes.
- Cover with aluminum foil and put aside in a warm place.
- Raise oven's temperature to 450°F.
- Arrange the mochi on a baking, placing the pieces at least 1½ inches apart.
- Bake for 8–10 minutes, or until puffed and brown.
- To serve, stack 4 pieces of mochi on a plate, then top with 1 tablespoon of pesto and 1 piece of salmon.
- Garnish with chopped parsley.

pesto sauce

What do you need?

2½ cups of chopped basil leaves
2 cloves of garlic
3 tablespoons of pine nuts
1 tablespoon umeboshi paste
2 tablespoons white miso
½ teaspoon salt
½ teaspoon ground black pepper
½ cup extra virgin olive oil

How to make?

• In a blender, mix the basil, garlic, pine nuts, umeboshi paste, white miso, salt, and pepper until a paste is formed.
• Drizzle extra virgin olive oil into the tube of the food processor until a smooth consistency is reached.

 Chef's Cooking Tip:

Mixing umeboshi paste and white miso simulates a parmesan cheese flavor.

Traditional Meatloaf with Red Crushed Tomato Sauce

Some recipes are better left as is. Familiar tastes are my definition of comfort food. At our house, this dish is a family tradition.

What do you need?
(Serves 10–12)

For the meatloaf:

1 pound ground turkey
1 pound ground beef
2 eggs
2½ tablespoons tomato paste
3 teaspoons salt
2 teaspoons turmeric
1 tablespoon paprika
½ cup gluten-free bread crumbs
1 onion, cubed
3 cloves of garlic, minced

For the tomato sauce:

1 (28 oz.) can crushed tomatoes
2 cloves of garlic, minced
1 small onion, chopped
1 teaspoon salt
½ teaspoon ground black pepper
1 teaspoon dry basil or oregano
1 tablespoon organic ketchup

How to make?

For the meatloaf:

- Preheat oven to 350°F.
- Sauté the onions until caramelized, add the garlic, and cook for another minute.
- Allow mixture to cool.
- In a large bowl, mix all the ingredients until thoroughly blended.
- Place the mixture into a 9" x 13" baking dish and shape into a long loaf.

For the sauce:

- In a small saucepan, mix all the ingredients together.
- Bring to a boil, and then cover and simmer over low-medium heat for 10 minutes.
- Allow the sauce to cool completely.
- Pour the sauce over the meatloaf.
- Cover with aluminum foil, making sure that the foil doesn't touch the meatloaf.
- Fill a second 9" x 13" baking dish halfway with water, and place it under-neath the first dish to prevent cracks while the meatloaf is cooking.
- Bake for 50 minutes.
- Remove aluminum foil and continue baking for another 45 minutes.
- Allow meatloaf to cool slightly before serving.

Crusted Baked Chicken

The maple buckwheat flakes give the crust a sweetness that will make your guests wonder what your secret ingredient is. I don't think you are in any way compromising flavor by baking the chicken instead of frying it; the ingredients are what supply the taste.

What do you need?
(Serves 4–6)

4 chicken drumsticks

4 bone in chicken thighs

2 cups plain rice milk or other milk substitute (not flavored)

1 large egg

2 cups crushed gluten-free corn flakes cereal

1 cup crushed gluten-free maple buckwheat flakes cereal

1 teaspoon salt

2 teaspoons garlic powder

3 tablespoons extra-virgin olive oil

canola oil spray

How to make?

- Preheat oven to 400°F. Spray baking sheet with canola oil.
- Pour the milk substitute into a bowl and allow the chicken to marinate, covered, for 20 minutes in the refrigerator.
- In a separate bowl, whisk the egg.
- In another bowl, mix the cereals, salt, and garlic.
- Dip chicken into the eggs, and then coat it with the cereal mixture.
- Transfer the chicken to a baking sheet and brush the chicken with extra-virgin olive oil.
- Bake for 45 minutes, or until golden brown.

Moroccan-Style Chicken

When we think about Morocco, we picture exotic scenes and foreign aromas. You may be inspired to belly dance around your kitchen when you experience the sweet smells of this chicken dish.

What do you need?

(Serves 4–6)

8 chicken cutlets (thighs or drumsticks)
2 tablespoons extra virgin olive oil
1 small chopped onion
2 cloves of minced garlic
3 tablespoons ground turmeric
2 tablespoons ground cinnamon
1 cup dried prunes
1 cup raisins
2 cups gluten-free organic chicken broth
salt
black pepper

How to make?

- Pat dry the chicken cutlets and season with salt and pepper.
- Heat a large and deep pan with the oil, sauté the onion and garlic for 5 minutes over medium heat.
- Add the chicken, prunes, raisins, and spices and cook for 5 minutes.
- Add the chicken broth and bring to a boil, then lower the heat and cook for an hour, covered.

Chicken Enchilada Delight

This is a very easy dish composed of affordable ingredients. You can serve it with guacamole, diced tomatoes, rice, and black beans.

What do you need?

(Serves 4–6)

For the enchiladas:

12 corn tortillas
1 small onion, diced
3 cups shredded cooked chicken
2 chopped garlic cloves
½ teaspoon cumin
1 teaspoon salt
½ cup shredded dairy-free cheese
canola oil

For the sauce:

1 (28oz.) can of organic crushed tomatoes
¼ cup water
1 teaspoon paprika
2 tablespoons canola oil
2 teaspoons salt
½ teaspoon ground black pepper

How to make?

- Preheat oven to 350°F.
- In a large pan, sauté the onion on medium heat for about 2 minutes.
- Add the garlic and cumin and cook for another minute.
- Allow the mixture to cool slightly.
- Using the same pan, mix the crushed tomatoes and water over medium heat.
- Add the paprika, oil, salt, and pepper.

- Bring to a boil. Cover with a lid and simmer for 15 minutes.
- Combine the chicken, the onion mixture, and half of the tomato sauce.
- Smear the bottom of an 8" x 8" baking dish with 4 tablespoons of the tomato sauce.
- Wrap the tortillas in a damp paper towel and warm them in the microwave for 30 seconds on high power.
- Add 1 tablespoon of the chicken and sauce mixture to the center of each tortilla.
- Fold the tortillas over the filling and roll to enclose it.
- Place the enchiladas in the baking dish and cover with the remaining tomato sauce.
- Top with shredded cheese.
- Bake uncovered for 30 minutes.

Chicken Breast Cutlets with Mushrooms and Dry Sherry Wine

This is a rustic dish with Italian flavor combinations. The earthy mushrooms, the moist chicken, and the sweetness of the sherry wine make this Italian-style dish perfect every time.

What do you need?

(Serves 2–4)

4 skinless, boneless, chicken breast cutlets

1 cup white rice flour

2 tablespoons extra virgin olive oil

3 cups halved button mushrooms

½ cup dry sherry wine

½ cup gluten-free chicken broth

2 tablespoons margarine

1 minced clove of garlic

2 teaspoons salt

2 teaspoons ground black pepper

3 tablespoons of chopped flat leaf parsley

How to make?

- Using a flat meat mallet, pound the chicken breasts until they are about ¼ inch thick.
- On a plate, mix the flour with 1 teaspoon salt and 1 teaspoon black pepper.
- Put the chicken in the flour
- Heat the oil in a large skillet; shake off all the excess flour.
- Arrange the cutlets in the oil and fry for 4 minutes on each side until golden, then remove the chicken from the pan.
- Using the same pan, sauté the mushrooms for 5 minutes until all the liquids have evaporated.
- Add the garlic, 1 teaspoon salt, and 1 teaspoon of black pepper.
- Pour in the wine in and let simmer for 2 minutes.
- Add the broth and the margarine and let simmer over medium heat for 5 minutes.

- Add the chicken cutlets to the pan and let simmer for another 5 minutes.
- Garnish with chopped parsley before serving.

Beef Stew with String Beans

What makes a good stew? It must have cubed beef beautifully cooked and accompanied by a perfect, thick sauce. The achievement of a great meal with almost no effort and the ease of just one big pot is a grand feeling.

What do you need?
(Serves 4–6)

3 pounds cubed beef (chuck or round)

1 large, chopped onion

4 minced garlic cloves

3 tablespoons tomato paste

3 cups gluten-free organic chicken broth

½ pound trimmed string beans

1 teaspoon curry powder

¼ cup olive oil

2 teaspoons salt

2 teaspoons ground black pepper

How to make?

• Pat dry the cubed beef and season with salt and pepper.
• In a large pot, brown the beef in batches.
• In the same pot, sauté the onion and garlic. Add the meat and tomato paste.
• Add the gluten-free broth, curry powder, salt, and pepper.
• Bring to a boil, lower the heat, and cover.
• Let simmer for 2½ hours, or until the meat is very tender.
• Add the string beans.
• Partially cover the pot and cook for another 30 minutes.
• Serve with basmati rice.

Meatball Kabobs

This recipe is inspired by my husband's cousin, Joseph. He used to make these kabobs for every occasion. After trying these jewels, you will wave good~bye to the eggs and the bread crumbs, traditionally used in kabobs. They taste great with tahini or hummus spread.

What do you need?
(Serves 4–6)

1 pound lean ground beef
¼ cup extra virgin olive oil
1 small halved onion
3 garlic cloves
¾ cup parsley
1/3 cup pine nuts
2 tablespoons dry dill
3 teaspoons turmeric
2 teaspoons salt
¼ teaspoon ground black pepper

How to make?

- Use food processor to process the onion, garlic, parsley, and pine nuts.
- Pour olive oil very slowly into the mixture to make a smooth paste.
- In a large bowl, mix the herb paste with the ground beef, dill, turmeric, salt, and black pepper.
- Spray a grilling pan or regular pan with canola oil.
- Grill the kabobs about 4 minutes per side.

Marinated Steak with Balsamic Vinegar and Soy Sauce

I am a great believer in relationships. If by now you haven't established a good relationship with your butcher, this is the time to go ahead and do so. The right cut of meat can make all the difference in the quality of your meal. This recipe requires a premium cut, such as tenderloin, filet, flank, or skirt, to accommodate the short cooking time involved in grilling. The steak goes well with baked potatoes, green salad, and steamed vegetables.

What do you need?

(Serves 4–6)

4 small beef steaks, 6 ounces each
2 teaspoons garlic powder
1 teaspoon salt
1 teaspoon ground black pepper
½ cup gluten-free soy sauce
2 tablespoons canola oil
4 tablespoons balsamic vinegar
1/3 cup honey

How to make?

- Pat the beef steaks dry. Rub the entire surface of the meat with garlic powder, salt, and ground black pepper.
- In a small bowl, Mix the soy sauce, oil, balsamic vinegar and place into a Ziploc bag with the meat.
- Marinate in the refrigerator for 30 to 60 minutes.
- Before grilling, take the meat from the refrigerator and let it stand for 15 minutes at room temperature.
- Remove the meat from the marinade.
- Heat grilling pan, and grill both sides of the meat 12–14 minutes for rare, 14–18 minutes for medium rare, or 18–20 minutes for medium.
- Allow the meat to rest for 10 minutes before cutting.

Grains, Pasta & Pizza

Creamy Risotto with Peas and Garlic

Risotto doesn't necessarily mean a lot of work. Make sure to use arborio rice, which absorbs liquids well, and to keep the liquids hot. The results will be creamy and tasty.

What do you need?
(Serves 4–6)

2 tablespoons extra virgin olive oil

1 cup chopped onion

2 minced garlic cloves

1 ½ cups Arborio rice

2/3 cup dry white wine

1 cup frozen peas, thawed

8 cups canned low sodium organic gluten- free chicken broth

1/3 cup grated dairy-free cheese

salt

freshly ground black pepper

How to make?

- Warm the broth in a saucepan and keep it warm over very low heat.
- In a heavy saucepan, add the extra virgin olive oil over medium heat.
- Add the onion, and sauté until translucent.
- Add the garlic, and cook for another minute.
- Pour the rice and stir for about 3 minutes.
- Add the wine, and cook until the liquid is absorbed, stirring often, about 3 minutes.
- Add 1 cup of hot broth and continue stirring often until the liquid absorbed.
- Continue to cook the rice over medium-low heat while adding the rest of the broth, stirring often. After about 30 minutes, the rice should be creamy and tender.
- Stir in the peas and the cheese.

Quinoa with Pine Nuts and Cranberries

Quinoa is an ancient grain. It contains all eight amino acids that build your body. I'm trying to include it whenever I can in my cooking. This recipe is light and very easy to prepare.

What do you need?

1 cup uncooked quinoa

2 tablespoons canola oil

½ teaspoon salt

½ teaspoon black pepper

2 cups gluten-free organic chicken broth or water

3 tablespoons cranberries

3 tablespoons pine nuts

How to make?

- In a medium saucepan, add the canola oil, quinoa, salt, and pepper.
- Mix well over medium heat.
- Add the gluten-free chicken broth or water and bring to a boil.
- Give it a quick stir, cover with a lid, and cook over low heat for 20 minutes.
- Remove from heat.
- Fluff the quinoa with a fork.
- Mix in the cranberries and pine nuts.

Stir-Fry Rice Noodles with Edamame and Red Bell Peppers

The first time I ate edamame was in an organic restaurant in Manhattan, where it was served as an appetizer with salt and sesame seeds. I just couldn't get enough of the delicious taste. This dish is the result of my experiments with edamame in my own kitchen.

What do you need?

(Serves 4–6)

For the stir-fry:

1 package of gluten-free stir – fry rice noodles or angel hair spaghetti
1 thinly sliced red bell pepper
1 cup frozen edamame (without the shells) defrosted and brought to room temperature
1 cup sliced green onions
2 tablespoons toasted sesame seeds

For the sauce:

3 tablespoons gluten-free soy sauce
1 tablespoon rice vinegar
6 tablespoons honey
½ teaspoon salt
½ teaspoon ground black pepper
1 teaspoon garlic powder

How to make?

- Cook the noodles according to the instructions on the box.
- Transfer the noodles into a big mixing bowl.
- Add the peppers, edamame, and green onions.
- In a small mixing bowl, mix the sauce ingredients.
- Pour the sauce over the noodles while they are still hot and sprinkle with toasted sesame seeds.

Pizza

Every cook has a few secrets up his or her sleeve. This recipe was my secret for several years. The combination of flours with the cider vinegar is what makes this dough so special.

What do you need?

For the pizza crust:

1 envelope of self-rising yeast
1 tablespoon sugar
¾ cup warm water
1 cup sweet white sorghum flour
1 cup tapioca flour
½ cup rice flour
2 teaspoons xanthan gum
2 teaspoons apple cider vinegar
1 stick of margarine, softened
1 teaspoon salt
1 egg
1 tablespoon extra virgin olive oil

For the tomato sauce:

1 tablespoon extra virgin olive oil
1(12oz.) can of crushed tomatoes
1 crushed garlic clove
1½ teaspoons salt
2 teaspoons paprika
ground black pepper

How to make?

To make the crust:

- Preheat oven to 400°F.
- Mix the warm water with the yeast and sugar until bubbles appear.
- In a big bowl, add the yeast mixture to the rest of the ingredients (omit the extra virgin olive oil) to form the dough.
- Spread 1 tablespoon of olive oil across the dough.
- Cover the bowl with a towel, and let the dough rise in a warm place for half an hour.
- Place the dough on a gluten free floured surface.
- Using a rolling pin, flatten and shape the dough into a 10-inch round pizza crust.

To make the sauce:

- In a medium saucepan, bring the olive oil and crushed tomatoes to a boil.
- Reduce heat to medium low, and mix in the rest of the ingredients.
- Simmer for 5–7 minutes, uncovered.
- Let the sauce cool completely and then pour over the crust.
- Sprinkle your favorite toppings (cheese, vegetables) over the pizza.
- Bake for 30 minutes or until the cheese melts and the crust is golden brown.

 **Chef's Cooking Tip:**

Try using this dough recipe to create your own delicious bread sticks. Roll the dough to a quarter-inch thickness, cut it into 1-inch-wide strips, and bake for 25 minutes at 400°F. Use the rich tomato sauce for dipping.

Vegetable Side Dishes

Baked Potatoes with Rosemary and Garlic

I love the flavor combination of herbs and potatoes. There is nothing better than coming home after a long day to indulge in a bowl of this goodness.

What do you need?

(Serves 4–6)

4 medium baking potatoes
¼ cup olive oil
4 cloves of crushed garlic
3 rosemary sprigs
2 teaspoons salt
½ teaspoon black pepper

How to make?

- Preheat the oven to 400°F.
- Cover a baking sheet with foil; set aside.
- Scrub potatoes thoroughly with a brush.
- Cut each potato lengthwise into eight wedges.
- Stir together the potatoes, olive oil, garlic, rosemary, salt, and pepper.
- Toss well until the potatoes are coated.
- Bake in the oven for an hour or until tender.

Potato Latkes

I remember the wonderful taste of the potato latkes my mother used to make for every occasion, especially Hanukkah. Instead of mashed potatoes, serve these potato latkes for a twist on an everyday meal.

What do you need?
(Serves 8–10)

5 large potatoes, peeled and shredded
4 tablespoons rice flour
5 eggs
3 teaspoons salt
1 teaspoon ground pepper
3 tablespoons chopped parsley
canola oil, for frying

How to make?

- Working in batches, enclose shredded potatoes in a clean cloth and squeeze to remove moisture.
- In a large bowl, mix all ingredients.
- Pour ½ inch of canola oil into frying pan and heat over a medium high heat about 4 minutes.
- Use single tablespoons of batter to form oval-shaped latkes and fry for about 4 minutes on each side until it golden brown.
- Serve with your favorite yogurt or applesauce.

Sugar Snap Peas with Garlic and Ginger

Sugar snap peas are crunchy and sweet. The addition of ginger and garlic makes this recipe extra special.

What do you need?

(Serves 4–6)

3 cups fresh sugar snaps peas

1 teaspoon grated ginger

2 tablespoons olive oil

2 minced cloves of garlic

½ teaspoon salt

½ teaspoon black pepper

How to make?

- In a small pot with a lid, boil 1 cup of water with ½ teaspoon of salt.
- Add the sugar snap peas, cover, and cook for 2 to 3 minutes.
- In a small pan, cook the ginger and garlic in hot oil for 2 minutes.
- Pour the sauce over hot peas, and season with salt and pepper. Serve immediately.

Broccolini with Balsamic Vinaigrette

Broccolini is an elegant vegetable with long stems and little green florets. Its distinctive taste is slightly bitter. The balsamic vinegar enhances the vegetable's flavor.

What do you need?

(Serves 4–6)

3 bunches of broccolini
¼ cup balsamic vinegar
2 minced garlic cloves
1 tablespoon honey
1 ½ teaspoons salt
½ teaspoon black pepper
½ cup olive oil

How to make?

- In a medium pot, boil 3 cups of water salted with 1 teaspoon of salt.
- Add the broccolini, do not cover, and cook for 3 minutes.
- Drain well. Remove from the pot; set aside.
- Mix together the balsamic vinegar, garlic, honey, salt, and pepper to make the vinaigrette.
- Slowly add olive oil to the liquid mixture until thoroughly combined.
- Pour vinaigrette over the warm broccolini and serve.

Broccoli Casserole

This casserole is another way to include vegetables in your family's diet. A slice of this dish packed in my son's lunch box makes both of us happy.

What do you need?

(Serves 6–8)

1 (10 oz.) package frozen chopped broccoli, thawed and well drained
1½ cups of garlic Tofutti cream cheese
3 eggs
1½ cup of rice milk
½ cup + 2 tablespoons grated rice cheese
2 teaspoons mustard powder
2 teaspoons garlic powder
½ cup gluten-free bread crumbs
2 teaspoons salt
1 teaspoon ground black pepper
2 tablespoons almond butter

How to make?

- Preheat oven to 350°F.
- In a large bowl, mix all ingredients except the 2 tablespoons of cheese.
- Pour the mixture into a loaf pan greased with canola oil.
- Top with the remaining grated cheese.
- Bake for 35 minutes or until golden brown.

Desserts

The Best Birthday Cake

This is a classic chocolate cake that's delicious and very easy to make. I bake it for every birthday celebration and other occasions that call for chocolate cake. You can add variety by using cake molds to produce different shapes. Refrigerating leftover slices will keep them fresh for several days.

What do you need?

For the cake:

2 cups sorghum flour
1¾ cups white rice flour
¼ cup tapioca flour
1 cup Dutch processed cocoa
½ teaspoon xanthan gum
1½ teaspoons baking soda
1½ teaspoons baking powder
1 teaspoon salt
1 cup canola oil
2½ cups sugar
4 large eggs
1 tablespoon instant coffee dissolved in two cups hot water
1 teaspoon vanilla extract

For the chocolate glaze:

6 ounces gluten and dairy free chocolate chips
2 tablespoons margarine
½ cup nondairy whipping cream

How to make?

- Preheat oven to 350°F.
- Lightly oil two 9" round or 15" x 10" baking pans.
- In a large bowl, combine the flours, cocoa powder, xanthan gum, baking powder, baking soda, and salt.
- In a separate bowl, combine the oil, sugar, eggs, vanilla, and coffee.
- Slowly stir the eggs mixture into the flour mixture until combined.
- Pour the batter into the pans. Bake for 25–30 minutes until a toothpick inserted comes out clean.
- Let the cakes cool completely before glazing.
- In a bowl placed on top of a saucepan of simmering water, melt the margarine, chocolate, and whipping cream together, stirring occasionally until the glaze is smooth.
- Remove the glaze from heat and cool down.
- Pour the glaze over the cooled cakes.

Peanut-Pecan Chocolate Cookies

What could ever go wrong when pecans, chocolate, and peanuts are involved? These cookies will melt in your mouth. You can make the dough and freeze it until you are ready to bake.

What do you need?
(Makes about 24 cookies)

1 cup organic creamy peanut butter
¾ cup sugar
1 large egg
½ teaspoon baking soda
¼ teaspoon salt
½ cup gluten and dairy free semisweet chocolate chips
¼ cup roasted chopped pecans

How to make?

- Preheat oven to 350°F.
- Mix all the ingredients together.
- Wet your hands to prevent sticking and form teaspoonfuls of dough into balls.
- Arrange on a baking sheet, leaving 2 inches between each cookie.
- Bake until golden brown for 13–15 minutes.
- Cool cookies completely on a rack.

Quinoa Cookies

In addition to its healthful properties, quinoa has a nice nutty flavor which blends well with the honey and cinnamon. This cookie is reminiscent of traditional oatmeal cookies.

What do you need?
(Makes about 25 cookies)

¾ cup quinoa flakes

1¼ cup white rice flour

2 teaspoons cinnamon

1 teaspoon baking powder

½ teaspoon xanthan gum

¼ teaspoon salt

1 stick of softened margarine

1 cup sugar

2 eggs

1½ teaspoons pure vanilla extract

4 tablespoons honey

¼ cup dry raisins

How to make?

- Preheat oven to 350°F.
- Line a baking sheet with a parchment paper.
- In a large bowl, mix the margarine, sugar, eggs, honey, and vanilla extract until thoroughly blended.
- In a second bowl, mix the quinoa flakes, rice flour, cinnamon, baking powder, xanthan, and salt.
- Add the eggs mixture to the flour mixture in three batches until thoroughly combined.
- Mix in the raisins.
- Refrigerate the batter for 10 minutes.
- Arrange the batter on the baking sheet in teaspoon-sized dollops, leaving 1-inch spaces between the cookies.
- Bake for 15–20 minutes.
- Cool cookies before transferring to a rack.

Nut Balls

I remember the first time I made these nut balls; they were so delicious I promised myself to double the quantity the next time. I love to take them with me when I'm traveling, they're my secret companion.

What do you need?

(Makes about 20 cookies)

1½ cup ground almonds
1 cup + ¼ cup powdered sugar
4–6 tablespoons cold water
1 teaspoon vanilla extract
2 teaspoons orange juice
½ cup unsweetened coconut flakes

How to make?

- In a bowl, mix the almonds, 1 cup of sugar, water, vanilla, and orange juice until thoroughly combined.
- Using a teaspoon, form the dough into balls.
- Roll the balls in the remaining sugar and then in the coconut flakes.
- Place the nut balls into decorative paper cups.

Tahini Cookies

Tahini is a sesame seed paste loaded with essential fatty acids. It has a nutty, sweet flavor. Kept in an airtight cookie jar, these healthy snacks stay fresh for weeks.

What do you need?
(Makes about 48 cookies)

2½ cups white rice flour

½ cup tapioca flour

2/3 cup sugar

½ teaspoon xanthan gum

1 stick margarine cut into small cubes

1 cup unseasoned raw tahini

½ teaspoon salt

3 tablespoons powdered sugar, sifted

How to make?

- Preheat oven to 350°F.
- In a food processor, mix the flours, sugar, and xanthan gum.
- Add in the cubed margarine, tahini, and salt and mix until thoroughly combined.
- Using a teaspoon, form the dough into round balls and flatten with your thumb.
- Arrange the cookies on a greased baking sheet.
- Bake for 15–20 minutes.
- After cooling completely, transfer to a cookie rack and dust with powdered sugar.

Cherry Clafouti

When you're in the mood for a great dessert that requires minimal effort, clafouti is exactly what the doctor ordered. I think of clafouti as an upgraded pancake. You can substitute pears, apples, or blueberries for the cherries.

How to make?

1 cup gluten free pancake mix
¾ cup soy milk or other milk substitute
2 eggs
2 tablespoons canola oil
2 tablespoons honey
3 tablespoons finely crushed almonds
2 cups pitted fresh cherries or thawed cherries
1 teaspoon vanilla extract
1 teaspoon grated lemon zest

How to make?

- Preheat oven to 375°F.
- Grease a 9-inch round pie pan with canola oil.
- In a large mixing bowl, combine all the ingredients except the cherries and set aside.
- Arrange cherries on the pan.
- Pour batter over the fruit.
- Bake for 45 minutes until puffed and light brown.
- Serve warm with your favorite ice cream.

The Most Delicious Chocolate Chip Cookies

I have tried many kinds of gluten-free chocolate chip cookies, but none of them come close to these. If you wish to store the dough, you can wrap it in plastic wrap and freeze for up to two weeks.

What do you need?

(Makes 24 cookies)

½ cup white rice flour
½ cup tapioca flour
½ cup sweet white sorghum flour
2 tablespoons quinoa flakes
1 teaspoon xanthan gum
¼ teaspoon salt
½ cup light brown sugar
1 stick softened butter flavored margarine
1 large egg
1 teaspoon vanilla extract
2 tablespoons honey
½ cup gluten and dairy free chocolate chips

How to make?

- Line a baking sheet with parchment paper.
- Preheat oven to 350°F.
- In a large mixing bowl, combine the flours, quinoa flakes, xanthan gum, and salt.
- In a separate bowl, combine the margarine and sugar.
- Add the egg, vanilla, and honey, and mix well.
- Add the egg mixture to flour mixture, and mix well.
- Mix in the chocolate chips.
- Arrange the dough on the baking sheet in teaspoon-sized dollops, leaving 1-inch spaces between the cookies.
- Bake for 20 minutes.
- Transfer cookies to a cookie rack when they have cooled completely.

Oatmeal Cookies

When it comes to oatmeal, it's important to use gluten-free oats. Beware of contamination. Check the list in this book to locate companies that manufacture gluten-free oats.

What do you need?
(Makes 30 cookies)

2½ cups gluten free oats
½ cup rice flour
1 cup light brown sugar
4 tablespoons maple syrup
3 large eggs
½ cup coconut oil
½ teaspoon baking powder
½ teaspoon baking soda
¼ teaspoon salt
1 teaspoon xanthan gum
1 teaspoon cinnamon

How to make?

- Preheat oven to 350°F.
- Lay parchment paper on 2 baking sheets.
- In a large bowl, mix all the ingredients together until thoroughly combined.
- Cover with plastic wrap, and refrigerate the mixture for 15 minutes to make the dough easier to work with.
- Arrange teaspoons-sized dollops of the dough on the baking sheet, leaving 1-inch spaces between the cookies.
- Bake 12–15 minutes.
- Allow cookies to cool completely before transferring to a rack.

Chocolate Truffles

These elegant little truffles work like a charm every time. I love to wrap them in a pretty container and give them as a gift.

What do you need?
(Makes about 30 truffles)

1 pound gluten and dairy free chocolate chips
1 cup parve heavy cream
1 tablespoon prepared coffee
1 teaspoon vanilla extract
½ cup sweetened coconut flakes
½ cup powdered sugar, sifted
½ cup chopped nuts

How to make?

- Heat the heavy cream in a saucepan and bring to a boil.
- Pour the cream through a fine sieve into a medium bowl.
- Add the chocolate, and mix well until everything is combined.
- Whisk in the coffee and vanilla extract.
- Refrigerate the mixture for 3 hours.
- Line a baking sheet with parchment paper. Scoop the batter into balls using a small ice cream scoop. Roll each chocolate ball in one of the toppings: nuts, coconut, or powdered sugar.
- Allow to cool for about two hours before eating.

Best Sugar Cookies

These wonderful sugar cookies hold their shape and taste great. No birthday party is complete without them. The icing is optional but adds color and festivity.

What do you need?

(Makes 24–30 cookies)

1 cup sweet white sorghum flour

1 cup tapioca flour

½ cup white rice flour

1 teaspoon xanthan gum

¾ cup sugar

2 sticks margarine,softend

1 large egg yolk

2 teaspoons vanilla extract

½ teaspoon salt

How to make?

- Preheat oven to 350°F.
- In a large bowl, mix together the sugar, margarine, egg yolk and vanilla extract until thoroughly combined.
- In another bowl, mix the flours, xanthan gum, and salt.
- Gradually pour the sugar mixture into the bowl of flour mixture.
- Mix until dough is formed.
- Form the dough into a log, wrap in plastic wrap, and refrigerate for 15 minutes.
- Roll the dough to ¼-inch thickness and cut into shapes with cookie cutters.
- Place cookies onto a baking sheet covered with parchment paper, and bake for 20 minutes until golden brown.
- Allow the cookies to cool completely before icing.

vanilla icing

What do you need?
(Makes about 2 cups icing)

2 cups powdered sugar, sifted
2 sticks margarine
2 teaspoons water
2 teaspoons vanilla extract

How to make?

- In a bowl, mix the margarine until softened.
- Add the sugar and then the water and vanilla. If the mixture is too dry add 2 tablespoons water.

Chef's Cooking Tip:

You can easily add food coloring to the icing. Make sure to buy organic coloring that contains natural vegetable extracts.

Chocolate Mousse

Warning: this mousse is addictive! Both kids and adults love it.
After a big meal, this is the perfect light dessert

What do you need?
(Serves 10–12)

1 cup gluten and dairy free chocolate chips
½ cup of coconut oil
1 tablespoon dry sherry
¾ cup sugar
4 eggs
½ teaspoon instant coffee
1/3 cup warm water
1 cup parve heavy cream

How to make?

• Melt the chocolate chips and the coconut oil over a double broiler of simmering water.
• Set aside to cool for 5 minutes.
• Add the sugar to the mixture.
• Add the eggs one by one.
• Mix well until all is incorporated.
• Add the sherry.
• Dissolve the instant coffee in 1/3 cup warm water and add to the mixture.
• In a separate bowl, whip the heavy cream until it holds soft peaks.
• Slowly mix the whipped cream into the chocolate mixture.
• Pour the mixture into individual serving cups.
• Cover and refrigerate for at least 2 hours.

Chocolate Fudge Cake

J've made this chocolate cake in the shape of a bunny, a bear, and even a butterfly. Jts texture is moist and holds its shape well. No one would guess it's also gluten and dairy free. This treat tastes even better the day after it's made.

What do you need?

For the cake:

2 cups white rice flour
1/3 cup soy flour
1/3 cup garbanzo flour
1 teaspoon xanthan gum
¼ cup cocoa powder, sifted
2 teaspoons baking powder
1 teaspoon baking soda
½ teaspoon salt
¾ cup sugar
¾ cup softened butter-flavored margarine
3 eggs
1 1/3 cups lukewarm water
½ cup vanilla coconut yogurt
½ cup dark corn syrup
1 tablespoon vanilla extract

For the chocolate icing:

2 cups gluten and dairy free chocolate chips
1 cup softened unsalted butter-flavored margarine
1¾ cup sifted powdered sugar
1 tablespoon dark corn syrup
1 tablespoon vanilla extract

How to make?

For the cake:

- Preheat oven to 350°F degrees.
- Grease one 10" x 15" cake dish or two 9" x 9" pans with canola oil.
- In a large bowl, mix the flours, xanthan, cocoa powder, baking powder, baking soda, and salt.
- In a separate bowl, mix the sugar, margarine, eggs, water, yogurt, corn syrup, and vanilla.
- Mix together the flour mixture and the egg mixture.
- Pour the batter into the pan.
- Bake for 55 minutes until a toothpick inserted comes out clean.
- Allow the cake to cool completely before icing.

For the icing

- Melt chocolate chips in the microwave for 30 seconds.
- Swirl and heat for another 30 seconds.
- Add the margarine and the powdered sugar, and mix well.
- Add the vanilla and the syrup until the mixture is glossy and smooth.
- Spread the icing over the top of the single-layer cake.
- For a double-layer cake, spread one-quarter of the icing on top one cake, then place the second cake on top and ice the top and sides.

Lemon Cheesecake

This cake is moist and not too dense. You can actually have more then one piece with no remorse. I love to add lemon to almost every dish. Like salt, it accentuates and defines other flavors. In this recipe, the water bath prevents cracks from forming on the cake, so don't skip that step.

What do you need?

8 ounces cookie crumbs (gluten and dairy free vanilla or ginger cookies)
1/3 cup butter flavored melted margarine
3 packages of dairy free cream cheese
1 cup sugar
4 large eggs
2 egg yolks
¾ cup fresh squeezed lemons

How to make?

- Preheat oven to 350°F.
- Grease a 9-inch round cake pan with canola oil.
- Mix the cookie crumbs into the margarine.
- Pour the mixture into the pan, pressing down to form a crust that lines the pan.
- Place the pan in the refrigerator to set.
- In a food processor beat the cream cheese until smooth.
- Mix in the sugar, eggs, and lemon juice.
- Remove the crumb-lined pan from the refrigerator and place inside a larger roasting pan.
- Pour warm water into the roasting pan, being careful not to spill into the crust.
- Pour the cheesecake filling over the crust.
- Bake for 50 minutes.
- Serve chilled.

Little Sunshine Cupcakes

These cupcakes light up my day, as their title indicates. I find myself baking them again and again, with glaze or without. I serve them at birthday parties or just when friends visit. But who really needs an excuse to enjoy a little cupcake?

What do you need?
(Makes 12 cupcakes)

½ cup tapioca flour

½ cup sweet sorghum flour

1 teaspoon baking powder

½ teaspoon baking soda

1 teaspoon xanthan gum

½ cup softened butter flavored margarine

2/3 cup sugar

2 large eggs

1 teaspoon vanilla extract

How to make?

- Preheat the oven to 350°F.
- Line a muffin sheet with 12 muffin papers.
- In a mixing bowl, mix the flours, baking powder, baking soda, and xanthan gum.
- In a second bowl, mix the margarine with the sugar, and then add the eggs and the vanilla.
- Add the eggs mixture to the flours mixture bowl, and mix well.
- Fill each muffin paper halfway up with the batter.
- Bake for 20 minutes until golden brown, and a toothpick inserted into the cupcake comes out clean.
- Allow the cupcakes to completely cool before frosting.

Brownies with Hot Chocolate Sauce

You can't have a party without brownies. This is my own version of the classic recipe. The chocolate sauce on top is optional, but in my house it is a must!

What do you need?

(Makes 16 brownies)

½ cup powdered sugar, sifted

½ cup cocoa powder

1 cup sorghum flour

1 teaspoon baking powder

1 teaspoon xanthan gum

1 cup canola oil

4 eggs

¾ cup sugar

¼ cup crushed walnuts

¼ cup gluten-free dairy-free chocolate chips

How to make?

- Preheat the oven to 325°F.
- Line a 9" x 9" baking pan with parchment paper, making sure the paper extends over the rims of the pan.
- In a big bowl, mix the powdered sugar, cocoa powder, flour, baking powder, and xanthan gum.
- In a second bowl, mix the, oil, eggs, sugar, walnuts and chocolate chips.
- Add the wet mixture into the flour bowl, and mix well.
- Pour the batter into the pan, and bake for 45 minutes, until a toothpick inserted into the cake emerges with just a few crumbs on it.

hot chocolate sauce

What do you need?

½ cup parve whipped cream
½ cup gluten and dairy free chocolate chips

How to make?

- Bring the chocolate chips and the whipped cream to a boil in a saucepan over low heat.
- Pour the sauce on top of the brownies while the cake is still warm.

Chocolate Cereal Bites

When my kids have a play date at our house, I pull out these four simple ingredients, and everybody has a good time playing and creating these chocolaty bites.

What do you need?

(Makes 20 bites)

1 cup gluten and dairy free chocolate chips
1 tablespoon coconut oil
1 teaspoon water
1 cup gluten and dairy free cereal flakes

How to make?

- Place the chocolate, coconut oil, and water in a medium stainless steel bowl.
- Balance the bowl on top of pot halfway filled with simmering water. Whisk until the chocolate melts (1–2 minutes)
- Remove from the heat.
- Add the cereal flakes, and mix well.
- Drop spoonfuls of the mixture into paper cups.
- Refrigerate for an hour.

Reader Resources

Internet sites for general information about gluten and dairy free living:

www.celiacdiseasecenter.org
www.celiaccenter.org
www.gluten.net
www.celiac.com
www.autism.com
www.celiactravel.com
www.glutenfreerestaurants.org

Internet sites for nutritional facts and information:

www.nutritiondata.com
www.fnic.nal.usda.gov/

Books:
The New Whole Foods Encyclopedia by Rebecca Woods
The All Natural Allergy Cookbook: Dairy-Free, Gluten-Free by Jeanne Marie Martin
Food and Healing by Annemarie Colbin
Celiac Disease A Hidden Epidemic by Peter H.R Green M.D. and Rory Jones
Traditional Foods are Your Best Medicine by Ronald F. Schmid
The Encyclopedia of Healing Foods by Michael Murray and Joseph Pizzorno with Lara Pizzorno

Bibliography

Autism Society of America. "Autism Society of America."
www.autism-society.org.

Gluten Intolerance Group. "Gluten Intolerance Group of North America." www.gluten.net.

Millward, C., and M. Ferriter, S. Calver, and G. Connell-Jones G. 2004. Gluten and casein free diets for autistic spectrum disorder. Abstract. Cochrane Database System Rev. (2): CD003498.

National Digestive Diseases Information Clearinghouse. "Celiac Disease Awareness Campaign from the National Institutes of Health."
www.celiac.nih.gov.

Vojdani, A, and T. O'Bryan, J. A. Green, J. McCandless, K. N. Woeller, E. Vojdani, A. A. Nourian, and E. L. Cooper. 2004. Immune response to dietary proteins, gliadin, and cerebellar peptides in children with autism. Abstract. Nutritional Neuroscience. (June 2004) 7(3):151–61.

Index

A

B

C

Q

Quinoa-47, 61, 71

R

Risotto-46
Rosemary-52

S

Salmon-32
Sauces-32, 34, 44, 75
Sherry wine-40
steak-
Marinated steak-44
String beans-42
Sugar snap peas-54
Sunflower Seeds-25

T

Tahini-7,63
Tempura-29
Toast-14
Tomato-34
Tortilla-16
Truffles-67

U

Umeboshi paste-8

V

Vanilla icing-69

Chef Einat Mazor is a certified chef from the Natural Gourmet Institute in New York City and is working as a restaurant culinary consultant and a caterer specializing in gluten and dairy free products.